Moments and Memories
The story of 1993 Berryessa Cougars

Anthony Lombardi

Mitt Madd Publishing—Murfreesboro,TN
Paperback ISBN: 979-8-9901628-0-8
eBook ISBN: 979-8-9901628-1-5
Title: Moments and Memories: The story of 1993 Berryessa Cougars
Author: Anthony Lombardi
Available formats: eBook
Paperback distribution

First edition

DEDICATION

I would like to thank my mom and my sister for always keeping me grounded, supporting me and loving me unconditionally.

To my wife who is my anchor, my puzzle piece and the greatest blessing God gifted to me.

To my incredible children, Dog Boy and Sweet P, every day is a blessing that I get to hug and give you kisses.

This story could not have been written without the contributions of those who ventured with me down memory lane. John North, Brandon Lattimore, JJ Dizon, Ken Pruitt and Darrel Thomas...thank you for going along with me on this journey and bringing our story to life.

MEMORY LANE

In the spring of 2023, I started unpacking from our move and going through old boxes. As with most people, when we do this we can't help but to reminisce as we dig through the boxes that reveal a bit a history from our earlier lives. I have a few boxes strictly dedicated to a particular time in my young life, my coaching years. As I dug through the bin filled with endless game tapes, old playbooks, trophies and pictures I came across a specific picture that when I looked at it, it was as if the floodgates of memories came crashing down on me. The team picture of the 1993 Championship from the Berryessa Cougars.

In 1993, the Berryessa Cougars 13 and 14 year olds (Midget Division) were the PAL Champions. Even though one can say it was only youth football; the dedication, effort, coming together as a team and overcoming adversity are the ingredients to which any and all championships occur regardless of what age and level the team competes at. Even the college teams and professional athletes have to deal with the same level of commitment and hard work in order to compete and win championships. There are no advantages or guarantees when competing against like teams with similar skills and physical attributes.

In 1993 the Florida State Seminoles beat Nebraska in the NCAA Championship and the Dallas Cowboys beat the Buffalo Bills to win the Super Bowl. If you'd ask any members of the Berryessa Cougars

1993 team they would recall that championship the same as Charlie Ward or Troy Aikman would recall theirs. How much hard work and effort they put in and the complete satisfaction of being crowned a Champion. Championships are championships and there only so many times in life when you compete in team sports that you can call yourself a champion. And that is a memory that will last with your forever.

As I'm staring down and this picture, I see the faces of the former players and coaches and aside from admiring, and depressed, that at 21 years old I was much thinner, had more hair and was better looking, I can't help but to smile and think fondly of that memorable season. Then the reality sets in, the year 2023 would be the 30 year anniversary for that team. This was my 2nd full year of coaching and my very first experience of winning a championship. Over my several years of coaching football I have won a few championships, but as they say, the first one always shares a special memory. Even though this was my first championship it holds a greater significance because of how that would set the direction and pathway for my life going forward. Not just for myself, but I'm sure for the other coaches and players as well.

I wonder what it would mean to search my old playbooks, watch some game films and maybe just start writing an essay or memoir if for nothing else for myself. Maybe I'll email my memoir out to some former coaches and players to bring them down memory lane as well. I started writing, and pretty soon a little more than just a couple pages started to flow out on my laptop so I decided to put it all together and share. Nothing special, just thought I liked it, so maybe it would be an interesting read for those who are similar in my age and have moments that they recall fondly from days of yesterday. This is my yesterday…this was my moment.

Chapter 1
Backyard Football

Let me start out and say honestly that I wasn't some exceptional athlete growing up. I typically was the smallest guy out there but you could consider me scrappy. To give you an example, when we'd play basketball they would call me Bobby Hurley. If you're not familiar with him, he was the point guard for the Duke Blue Devils. He wasn't a particular gifted athlete, but he had what you'd call moxie, he wasn't afraid to mix it up and he always kept coming at you. This pretty much was the type of kid I was when I played sports.

I remember when I first started playing football in the 6th grade for the Berryessa Cougars. I was one of the littler guys but I was faster than most and could hold my own against the bigger players. I started both years I played. I moved my 8th grade year and played at Reed Middle School. That was the first time I experienced the negative impact a coach can have on a young impressionable kid. During the drills I would surprise the other players at how I was able to tackle and not shy away from the better players. This one day at practice, the coached moved me to outside linebacker. I never played this position before, I usually played corner. I remember this play like yesterday. At the time I didn't know what to call the play, but after my years of coaching experience I can now tell you it was a sweep with the fullback lead blocking on the edge.

Before the coach moved me, I had been playing the corner back position. I was taught to go wherever the wide receiver went and tackle him when he gets the ball. Not exactly brain surgery, and later I would learn was pretty sad coaching. I bring this up because when the ball was snapped the fullback was coming at me, I just followed and ran with him because that's what I was doing at corner. Now obviously looking back on this, and as I've taught my players, I should have taken the angle and blown up the fullback to either get to the running back or at least open it up for another teammate to make the tackle.

So how did this one play affect me? After the safety came in to the make the tackle the coach ran directly to me and yelled in my face using every 4 letter word. But most of all, I could only hear the words "you're a stupid dumbass idiot, why would you do that?" After he was done yelling at me I just felt like was I worthless. Being a 13 year old, who loved just playing the game, I still didn't know the ins and outs of the game aside from having Walter Payton, Ronnie Lott and Eric Dickerson posters on my wall.

I was crushed. This was the first time I can recall a coach ever yelling at me and more importantly, all my teammates were looking at me and all I can feel is embarrassed. After that practice I still stayed on the team, but something changed inside of me. I didn't want to be yelled at again or embarrassed in front of my teammates, my friends. So I became a wallflower and didn't want to put myself in that position. The funny thing is, on the weekends my friends and I would bring our equipment home so we could play "backyard football". I loved it, and back in the day when we would choose up teams, I was typically one of the first players chosen because I was fast, could run the ball and could tackle.

After that school year, I moved back to California for my Freshman year and like back in Missouri I developed friendships with the neighborhood guys and we'd play football at the park. And just like when I played with my friends back in Missouri, I was usually one of the top guys picked. My new California friends all played for the Freshman team and they kept telling me to come out for the team. I loved playing with them at the park, after school or on Saturdays, but I just didn't want to play for the high school football team. I can't help but to believe that that one play when the coach at Reed Middle School just crushed my spirit. Looking back, I'm confident I would have made the team and been a key contributor if not a starter. Not because of arrogance, but because my friends that I played with at the park were all starters on the team and if I could compete with them at the park, I'm sure I could have competed with them on the field as well.

After my Freshman year, I moved back to Missouri to live with my mom and finish High School. Most of my friends played football for the High School team. And just as before we would always play on the weekends, but without equipment because I didn't have any. This became a ritual and before you know it, we were playing full on 11 on 11 and guys standing on the sidelines to be subbed in. It kept growing to where guys from other schools and even adults would start to come. This became a pretty big thing. Even though the numbers grew, when we chose up teams, I would still be one of the top few guys to be chosen.

Finally my Senior year, I decided to play for the football team. Even though we would still play our Saturday games, for some reason I wasn't the same player on the football field as I was at the park. At the park all I did was play and have fun. On the field at practice I seem to always revert back to that memory and didn't want coaches to yell or embarrass me. There's a saying that you can't be disappointed if you don't try, well I simply chose not try. I'm not going to say I would have been a star or even a starter in High School, all I'm saying is my mental confidence paralyzed me from even believing I could compete and just play. The memory of that one fateful day when I was 13 years old still haunted me.

Chapter 2
Impactful Moments

This reflection down memory lane is to give a brief description as to what inspired me to get into coaching. After high school I moved back to California. Like all of us do in our adolescent years, we ask the question of "who am I and what am I doing with my life". I remember looking for a job through the newspaper (yes back in those days) and I saw this job posting to work with kids at the YMCA. I thought about that and decided that working with kids would be easy and fun. After I had been working for a few months, there was this little girl name Lisa. She was 6 at the time. We were outside on the playground and she came up to me on the bench and sat next to me. She said "Mr. Anthony I like you." Being the good counselor I was, of course I responded "I like you too". But then she went further and said this "No I really like you, you make me feel good".

This isn't hyperbole, this conversation really happened. This 6 year old said these profound words to me and it changed my outlook on life forever. At this time I was 20 years old and my goal was to be the next Edward Lewis from "Pretty Woman" and build a real estate empire. But after this conversation, I didn't want a job to make millions of dollars and be rich, I wanted to work with kids and try to make a positive difference in their life. So now, I was finally able to answer the "who am I" question. I found my passion and I knew my life's mission…I wanted to work with kids.

One day on my way home from work at the YMCA I drove past a park and I saw a PAL (like Pop Warner) football team practicing. I recognized the team immediately, the maroon and gold Berryessa Cougars. It was the first team I ever started playing organized football for and also my best memory of playing football. I pulled into the parking lot and just watched for a bit. I loved football and now I knew I loved working with kids so I thought it would be great to give coaching a try. I got up the nerve and asked one the coaches about volunteering as a coach. I was pointed in a direction to Coach King. He said I could work with his team, they were the younger guys (9/10 year olds).

I just wanted to be around and see if I could fit in and not be a distraction. Even though my "on field playing" experience was limited I understood the game. It was only a few practices and then Coach King came to me and said the Jr. Midgets (11/12 year olds) coaching staff just quit and asked if I wanted to coach them. Here I am, all of maybe a 2 week experience of coaching and they ask me if I wanted to run the defense for the team, naturally I jumped at the opportunity.

I didn't know too much of anything drill wise or calling plays so I made a lot of stuff up. I developed a relationship with the players, probably because I was not much older than them, but also I'd imagine because they felt like I respected them. The one thing I made sure to not do was to curse at them and especially not call them names or embarrass them. I'm all too familiar with what that can do to a kid.

I didn't have any younger brothers so in a sense I looked at these young guys as a younger brothers or nephews.   I had fun and I bet if you'd ask those players, even though we weren't very successful, they would say they had fun.   I felt for them because similar to me growing up, I felt abandoned. For the rest of the season I coached the defense and another coach did the offense.

I was learning on the fly, gaining experience with drills and planning for practices. I'm getting game experience of actually calling plays and this is when I discovered the coaching bug.   There is something different about being on the sidelines and watching your players do things you've been coaching them to do. Getting excited when the players would make a great or I'd pick them up when they made mistakes. But most importantly I was having a fun, kind of like my fond memories of playing at the park. Honestly, just as with being a counselor, I could say I was a natural with coaching. Not X and O's or calling plays or being some sort of genius with game planning. The relationship part came easy and instinctual to me. Which I would later learn is the most important part to becoming successful in coaching.

Similar to that conversation with 6 year old Lisa, I believe the players responded to me because of how I made them feel about themselves.   The season finished and I can't tell you what our record was but we did win a couple games. But I was hooked....I couldn't wait til the next season and just hoped that I would get the opportunity, which thankfully happened and that experienced changed my life forever.

Chapter 3
The Foundation…1992

The season of 1992, Coach Ken Pruitt welcomed me to his coaching staff. Coach Pruitt was the head coach and his brother Ricky was on the staff as well, along with a few other coaches. I'm not exactly sure the position Ricky coached, but I'll refer to him as the "advisor" which you'll later understand why. The Defensive Coordinator was Coach Dave. I coached the Linebackers, Coach Pablo did the Defensive Backs and Larry Lee coached the Defensive Line. Coach Pablo and Larry Lee were brandy loving older experienced coaches and they would take this young cocky kid under their wings. Coach Pablo's son played on the team but he wasn't one of those typical dads that only was there to coach his kid, he actually coached for several years and I would lean on his knowledge and experience to help my growth as a coach. He and I meshed together because he tolerated my lip and I think because I would always make him and Larry Lee laugh.

My first experience with Coach Pruitt was at our first coaching meeting. I remember sitting in the living room with a staff of like 7 other coaches and listening to Coach Pruitt. He has a calm presence but also had a no nonsense demeanor. I could tell right away he is a profound leader. I'm sure he has or is a leader of organizations he is involved in. Also I'm sure he has an interesting past that I'll touch on later. Anyways, during this meeting, me being the young cocky 20 year old, spoke up in the meeting and said something like "why are you the head coach, what is it that you do to be the head coach."

The room turned quiet and the other coaches (all older and obviously wiser) just shook their head in disbelief that I would say this at a coaching meeting, especially my first meeting. I guess I came across as challenging him, which I would later learn was not the thing to do. Pruitt tilt his head and looked at the other coaches like "who the hell does this kid think he is". But being the graceful, thoughtful and stoic person he is, he simply said "We focus on details and winning is a byproduct of what we do well". I don't know why, but that comment would become a philosophy that I would carry the rest of my coaching years as well into my life in general. It really stood out to me.....the game itself is won by the paying attention to the little things. Winning isn't the focus, the details are what you focus on, and that's how you become a winner.

Funny story, the following year when Coach Pruitt and I were talking about that moment, he made sure to tell me that if it wasn't for his brother Coach Ricky, that that was going to be my last day on his coaching staff. He said "I was going to fire your ass" and that Ricky told him that "I'm just a little shit that doesn't know any better." Which I can't disagree with.

When I first starting coaching I was hooked. There was just something about being on the practice field and on the sidelines during the game. This was a different kind of intensity that I haven't felt before. I was fully immersed with coaching. I loved watching film of upcoming opponents and trying to game plan to stop their offense. I finally felt like I was part of something, part of a team that was much different than growing up and just playing the game. With the guidance and tolerance of Coach Pruitt, he put up with my lip and cockiness, he welcomed me and made me feel like I belonged. Thank god he didn't fire me after that meeting. Without sounding over exaggerated, I can honestly say that had I not met Coach Pruitt, my life would have been drastically different. It's funny how a person can come into your life at a particular time when you need them the most. Coach Pruitt used football as a means of changing lives, not just the players but everyone that was a part of his teams and especially me

.

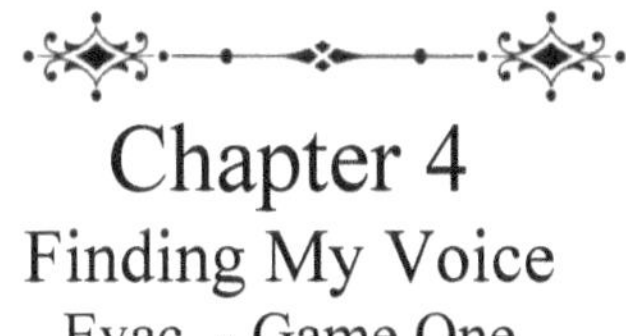

Chapter 4
Finding My Voice
Eyac - Game One

I remember early in the season at a coaching meeting we were playing the EYAC Crusaders who were undefeated at the time. They had a Tight End who was big and fast and was unstoppable from the film I was watching. I was looking forward to the meeting because I spent the whole time game planning for the defense. Even though I wasn't the Coordinator, I thought I had a good game plan that would help slow him down. As we watched the film, I highlighted plays on the film and pointed out that on the plays he caught passes he would line up off the line of scrimmage and get a free release. My game plan was simple. I thought we should double team at the line of scrimmage and hit him to slow him down. Also, we should move Dizon to his side because he was our best linebacker and guard him 1 on 1.

Going into the game I felt proud of myself for coming up with a game plan and confident we would do well in the game. By this time me, Coach Pablo and Larry Lee have formed a great bond. Usually because we thought Coach Dave was a dumbass and hated his shitty defense. Well needless to say, Coach Dave didn't agree with the suggestion and instead kept the lame defense we'd been using all season long. Well as usual, his game plan didn't work....the tight end got free and he scored on 2 long TD passes on their first 2 possessions.

This is where the other Coach Pruitt, Coach Ricky "advisor", came into play. Instead of coaching and keeping my head in the game, I walked to the end of our sideline. I isolated myself and literally took a knee, began to sulk and pout like a baby. I took it personal that my voice wasn't heard and I didn't know how to handle it. Coach Ricky didn't really speak too much but by this time I've learned that when he spoke you'd better listen. He was a no nonsense guy that I'm sure has spent some time behind bars for breaking heads, but I'm also sure it would've been justified because the other person probably deserved to get his ass kicked. I felt that he and Coach Pruitt where in lock step and Coach Pruitt didn't need to say much, he'd just give Ricky the look and Ricky knew exactly what to do.

Coach Ricky strolled over to me. He stared down at me with his stone cold eyes and said "get your little ass up and get back over there and coach". It was what I needed to hear and he definitely told me. I look at both the Pruitt's as mentors and coaches not just for the players but for myself as well. I'm still just barely 20 and learning about being a man and at that moment I was given a very valuable lesson. You never quit and show your emotions when things don't go your way, and more importantly to adhere to the words of Coach Ricky or my ass was his. There is another story about Coach Ricky and Coach Pruitt that I'll share later...

We battled through the season fortunately we made the playoffs. But unfortunately or our first game we would play the same undefeated team that kicked our ass earlier in the season, EYAC. We prepared for the game knowing full well that we were the underdog and it would take a herculean effort to pull off the upset. This was my first experience coaching during the playoffs and even though my emotions always ran high, I was at a totally different intensity level. I love the playoff atmosphere. It doesn't matter what level you play or coach at or what sport it is. Anytime you get the chance to put it all on line with a winner take all scenario you have got to embrace the moment. I never understood the term "the lights are the brightest in the playoffs", but I do now.

We start the first half and it was déjà vu all over again. Just like in the first game, they jumped on top of us early by scoring 2 long touchdown passes to that damn Tight End. By this time in the season, Coach Pablo and I developed a really good relationship in which he kind of looked out for me because I would usually say or do stupid shit. But he loved it because I would always make him and Larry Lee laugh. I'm sure they looked at me like a little brother or nephew that was just learning his way. Coach Pablo helped me learn more about defense and the nuisances of coaching, like making sure to always have fun.

We would always talk throughout practices and in the games and were like 2 minds melded together. Our one common bond was we hated the defense that Coach Dave called. He was passive and wouldn't listen to us so we did what most coaches do, we talked shit and bitched behind his back…well mostly me, Pablo and Larry Lee just laughed and let me vent.

So now we're playing the same team and the game starts out exactly the same as last time. But this time I learned from my previous experience when Coach Ricky told me to "get my little ass up and go coach". By now I was all in and was committed to coaching and to do anything to win games. I didn't isolate myself or start pouting but instead Pablo and I were both pissed. Here we are in the playoffs and we keep doing the same things as before and Dave wouldn't listen to us. We're not making adjustments or anything and we're allowing the same thing to happen.

Luckily we went to halftime only down 13 – 0. With Pablo by my side I went directly to Coach Pruitt and I told him "I can stop this". I don't know where that came from. For some reason I felt the courage and fight to speak up not for myself but for the players and the team. I was frustrated and pissed that we are letting the same damn thing happen again and our season is going to come to an end if we don't fix it. He looked at Pablo and then at me eye to eye and asked "you can stop this?" This time I was emphatic with more courage and confidence said "yes, I know how to stop them." Coach Pruitt tilted his head back, looked at me with his eyes in a way I can only describe as "ok kid, don't screw it up." He simply said "you got it."

I'm not sure how I developed that courage or confidence or even why Coach Pruitt put that trust in me but he made that change on the fly right there at half-time. I have always viewed Coach Pruitt as a mentor because I truly believe he saw something in me that I didn't see and he gave me the confidence to believe in myself. As I mentioned before, the Pruitt's weren't just coaches of players but of men as well.

When Coach Pruitt handed me the reigns, Coach Pablo and I were all over it. Looking back I'm sure when Coach Pruitt looked at Pablo, he trusted that Pablo was supporting me. Coach Pablo always had my back, no matter how much trash I talked or trouble I got into he'd always be there to support me. He wouldn't get upset or frustrated with me, instead he and Larry Le would always laugh at my antics. I can still hear him laughing and saying "Lombardi what are you doing or Lombardi you can't do that". But in this instance, with his support and without him saying it, I can visualize and hear him saying "Lombardi you can do this, I got your back".

It's like I've been preparing for this moment all season and now I finally had my chance so I better not screw it up. Pablo and I already knew what to do. We were going to be more physical and slow them down by putting more pressure on them at the line of scrimmage. Basically the exact same game plan we should've done the first time we played them.

We started the 2nd half and the defense was on-point. We were blowing them up and playing physical defense like we haven't seen all season. Our offense started to get going and we scored 2 touchdowns (but missed the extra points) so we were still behind. Late in the 4th quarter we just scored and they had the ball around their own 20 yard line. We stuffed them on 1st and 2nd down and after both plays we had to call our timeouts to preserve the clock. By this time the game clock was down to a little more than 2 minutes remaining.

It was 3rd and 9 and I remember this so vividly that to this day it still drives me crazy. If you ask Coach Pablo he would say the exact same thing. What made our defense successful in the 2nd half was we were being physical without blitzing.   Here we are, underneath the lights and all the momentum late in the 4th quarter. Everything was thick with emotion and you can feel the energy in the air.   The atmosphere was getting crazy with our sidelines and the crowd was yelling, "DEFENSE… DEFENSE…. DEFENSE…" We have turned the game around and are on the brink of getting the ball back, pulling off the upset and knocking off the undefeated #1 seed.

EYAC breaks the huddle and our boys are getting in position, crowd stomping on the bleachers and yelling, "DEFENSE…DEFENSE". The Tight End lines up nearest our sideline and our defense lines up like we have been doing the entire second half. All of the sudden I see Dizon walk up to the line and he is outside of the Tight End. I look over to Coach Dave and he's telling him to blitz.

Because we made the adjustment at half-time, we shut down EYAC and they couldn't move the ball. The whole 2nd half, Coach Dave didn't say anything but now when it comes down to the biggest play of the game he tells our best player to blitz???? By the time I yell "DIZON GET BACK" it was too late. The ball had snapped and wouldn't know it….they called the perfect play at the perfect time…Pop Pass. Because Coach Dave decided to blitz Dizon, the Tight End got a free release and was wide open. It was a simple quick pass to the Tight End who caught the pass for 10 yards.

They picked up the first down and ran out the clock. Pablo and I were beyond pissed and we went off on Dave with a variety and creative use of the famous 4 letter words. Even though Coach Pruitt was stoic I could tell he was pissed but of course Coach Ricky didn't hold back and pretty much said what the whole coaching staff was wanting to say…"What the @$% are you doing Dave!!!"

Even though the frustration for the way the season ended, I learned the valuable lesson of never quitting, picking yourself up and pressing forward and most importantly….never blitz on 3 and long!!!

Chapter 5
Unity Prayer

I became all in with coaching and loved every aspect of it. From the comrade, to practice planning, watching film but most of all, I became addicted to the competition. There is something different about competing as a player versus competing as a coach. I remember going into games I couldn't sleep the night before. I would constantly be writing notes, looking at our roster and game planning. As a player you are focused in on your specific task, but as a coach you're the General leading your troops into battle. You focus on the entire picture and figure which buttons to press and not press. It really is an addiction.

During the 92' season I started to develop my voice I would get visions of plays and think of what I would say or speeches to tell the team. One day I'm in my car and these words came across my head. I'm not sure how it started but it was like a chant and as I started putting the words together I could hear myself telling the players and before I knew it I was yelling at the top of my lungs this chant….I had actually given it a name "The Unity Prayer".

I can't tell you which game it was, but it was early in the season. The night before one of the games I asked Coach Pruitt if I could lead the team in a prayer. He said he wanted us to practice it first. That

Friday night I took the team by myself and I told them to join hands and repeat after me.

"This is my brother, together we unite"...they repeated.
"To go into battle, to onto fight"…..they repeated.
"We step on the field and dig our cleats in the grass,"…..they repeated.
"To blood to sweat to tears,"...they repeated.
"And to Kick Some Ass!!!"…they repeated.

And with that the team erupted. It had a greater effect than I could even imagine. We yelled "kick some ass" so loud that the other coaches heard us. For dramatic effect I would pause before saying the last line, just to let it build up. To this day, I bet if you ask any of the players they would remember the prayer. Needless to say, from that day forward Coach Pruitt let me be in the end zone with the team and lead us out by the Unity Prayer. It became our war chant…out rallying cry.

RENO BOWL GAME

After we loss to EYAC in the playoffs, the team would travel to Reno for a bowl game. Unfortunately I couldn't attend because I was already flying out of town. So the night before they were to leave we were at the pizza parlor and since I wasn't going to be able to lead the team onto the field, Coach Pruitt told me to do the Unity Prayer right there in the restaurant. So for the last time that season I led them in the Unity Prayer.

They went on to Reno and in fact would play and beat a team that was older than them. When they returned, as usual we all celebrated at the pizza parlor. The players were excited and Coach Pablo told me "Lombardi we did it". And I said I know it's awesome that we won. He looked at me, smiled and said "No Lombardi, we did the Unity Prayer for you." I can't describe how much that affected me. I felt an enormous sense of pride that they would still want to do that and even more so, let me know they did.

What was so special about that team is we were young but we had this sense of belief and were already looking forward to the next season. The 1992 team that would lose a heart break in the playoffs, go on to win a Bowl game and be ready to embark on one of the most memorable experiences they would have in their young lives. And yes, the Unity Prayer would lead us onto the field for every game.

Chapter 6
"WINNING IS A BY PRODUCT"

I was driven to coaching because I truly felt I wanted to make a positive lasting impression to the players. I know firsthand how a player can be impacted positive or negatively and how their spirits can be crushed. My philosophy was to make them believe they can achieve more than they thought they could. I'm not going to say I never used bad words, but the one thing I can promise you is I never used language in a demeaning or disrespectful way. I never wanted to break a player's spirit, instead I wanted to build players up not break them down.

I looked at the players as myself and thought how was I when I was their age? I was an impoverished kid from a divorced background who didn't have any relationships or guidance from my father, uncles or any positive men until years later. I was a troubled kid, just ask my sister… When I was really young I had some unfortunate stuff happen to me that took many years of counseling to get over it. I only bring this up because I would always wonder about the background of these kids. Who went home to an alcoholic or drug abused parent? Who went home to no parents? Who would get a beating, wouldn't eat or even have a bed to sleep in? These are the realities of the kids that we coached.

This was a characteristic and philosophical belief I developed with coaching. When I eventually became a head coach this would be the foundation for all my teams and coaches. I think I finally understood what Coach Pruitt told me that one day "Winning is a byproduct of what we do well." It's not just the details of coaching drills on the field. It's the details of getting to know your players, their background and to build respect and trust. To let them know that you believe in them, not just as a football player but as a young person. It's not about developing the relationship for those 2 hours at practice, it's the relationship you build beyond the football field. It's driving them to and from practice, getting them something to eat because you know their hungry. Asking them about how they are doing at home or school and sincerely want to know. The byproduct to winning is not just focused on the scoreboard, but true winning is building a real relationship and instilling the belief that the players can do anything not just on the field but in life in general.

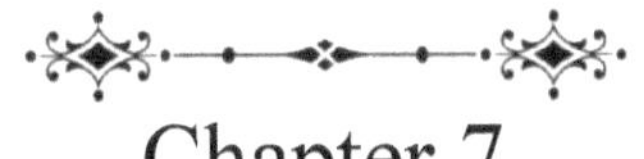

Chapter 7
LIFE CONVERSATION…MY BROTHER LEE

Before the 1993 Season started, I went back to Missouri to visit my friends and family. This trip had another impact on me that would help guide my life forever. My older brother Lee was a very calm person but with a serious demeanor. He was what you'd describe as a keen observer of people and had an in-depth philosophy of the human spirit.

He would love to get into deep meaningful conversations with you about yourself and about life in general. He was a great listener who really wanted to hear what you had to say and what seemed to be at the perfect time, he would drop some advice that if you listened, could change your life.

One night we're at the bar playing pool and this is the first time I can recall anyone talking to me man to man and really wanting to hear about my thoughts about life. Here I was sharing a drink with my older brother who I idolized and we were just shooting pool and talking like men. I was excited talking about my experience coaching and working at the YMCA and that I finally felt like I had a purpose in life. He was genuinely interested and would ask me questions to keep me talking and sharing my passion.

At some point during this conversation I brought up the disapproval conversations I had with my dad and others. The discussion would usually sound something like "coaching isn't a real thing, it's just a hobby." Or "You'll need to find something else to do with your life"…..blah blah blah. These comments would have similar effects as to the 8th grade coach at Reed Middle School that would make me question myself, cripple my spirit and just like when I was 13 years old would start to feel worthless.

My brother was getting ready to shoot when he heard me say this. He turned towards me, dropped his stick to his side and looked right at me. He simply asked me "Do you enjoy what you're doing?" and I told him "yes". Then he told me, "If you enjoy what you're doing then who gives a shit what anyone else thinks". "You just keep coaching and doing what you love and you'll be great." And then with another profound statement that has forever changed my outlook on life he said "life isn't about money, it's about doing something you love."

As usual, when my brother Lee gave advice it was specific and direct to the point. I've always looked back on this conversation as one that not only changed my trajectory in life, but also gave me the words of support and encouragement to follow my passions. He didn't just talk to me as a little brother, he talked to me as a man. He talked with me with love in his heart.

Chapter 8
PRESEASON

July rolled around and the beginning of the season was upon us. We started the preseason workouts and practices and there was a sense of newness and excitement. Most of our players had returned and then a few more players that would become key pieces to our championship run joined our team. As well, the majority of our coaching staff remained the same but with one addition, Coach Darrel Thomas. Coach Darrel and I meshed together right away. He was not too much older than me, he shared the same love for talking trash, chasing women and partying. Not to mention he became the only other white guy on the staff so I wasn't alone.

Part of the love of coaching is the camaraderie you build amongst the other coaches. Even though we were part of a staff of older, wiser and most importantly tolerant men, they looked out for us the same as an Uncle or Older brother would do. Naturally, part of the camaraderie is talking trash and so of course the coaches would give us the nickname as the "Vanilla Brothers" or the "Siamese Twins". It's not a coincidence that we would later become like brothers the rest of our lives. We would party together, laugh together, fight together, cry and lean on each other and be groomsmen for each other's wedding.

We were inseparable on and off the field but especially during games. We literally would almost instinctively be standing right next to each other and if I wasn't making the play call he'd be doing it. I'm not sure if we just naturally gravitated towards each other or if Coach Pruitt told Darrel to stand next to me to keep me from running onto the field. I had a tendency of getting so focused that I would start to drift off our sidelines and sometimes be like 5 yards on the field. Darrel would always have my back, like literally yelling at me "Tony get back" or grabbing me by the shirt to pull me back so we wouldn't get a penalty. We naturally fed off each other and as the game got more intense, which usually started in the locker room, Darrel and I just locked it in from the get go.

Along with the other key players to join the team, Coach Darrel became the final ingredient to make us the perfect team. With Coach Pablo and Larry Lee not only did all 4 of us become the perfect group, Pablo and Larry Lee had even more reason to laugh whenever Darrel and I would do stupid shit, which happened quite often. Together the 4 of us would create the most dominate defense the league has ever seen before.

Chapter 9
In the Words of Coach Darrel
This chapter was written by Coach Darrel Thomas…

It was 1993. I was going through a pretty tough divorce and I needed to keep my mind from going crazy, so thought, hey, I love football, why not try and become a coach! Next day I opened the newspaper and wouldn't you know I saw an ad for coaching "PAL Football coach needed for Berryessa Cougars" and said to contact Coach Ken Pruitt.

Finally, after trying for about 2 weeks, I was able to speak with Coach Pruitt. He told me to meet him at the pizza place off of Berryessa. Now, I lived on west side San Jose, and I had never been to the "Eastside". Let's just say, I wanted to get in and out of there as quick as I could. But I walked in and Ken was already there, with a pitcher of beer and 2 glasses. We shook hands and talked for hours about life and football. I knew right away he and I were going to hit it off. He had a very calming way of talking to you with his quick jerks and "hey did you know…" sound offs. He was a hoot! Then he said, now we just promoted a coach from last year to be our new Defensive Coordinator… His name is Anthony Lombardi…and I want you to meet him.

This is where it gets crazy! I remember Ken set up another meeting with Tony, me and his brother Rick at the pizza place. So, I hauled my ass back over there, and Ken and Rick were there with pitchers of beer already on the table. But Tony was late…which I would learn to become as usual.

I remember he walked in and Ken goes there's Lombardi. I turned around and I looked right past him because all I remember was seeing a kid who looked like he was 15 years old with a cocky, shitty grin! But BOOM, it was Lombardi!!!!!!! I laughed my ass off – internally… I thought THIS guy is going to be the Defensive Coordinator? But, you know, we hit it off from the get go – I knew I was going to have fun coaching with this dude…. We were both high energy, and we both knew football….our strategy was simple – make sure the kids know their assignments, be aggressive and the rest will fall into place.

So, the first defensive coaching meeting was at Lombardi's house. Again, heading ALL the way over to the Eastside of San Jose… I remember meeting Larry and Pablo.   2 cats that were absolutely HYSTERICAL!!!! Those dudes NEVER stopped pounding on Lombardi… just ripping him from head to toe when Tony was presenting the "defense" for the year… I felt bad for the little guy, but I saw what Tony was doing, and I knew our defense was going to be NASTY!   Here was this little shit that maybe weighed 120lbs telling grown men what to do and he would dish it out as much as they gave him. I loved it…and I think Pablo and Larry did to. I think the coaches just wanted to make sure we knew what we were doing…. And we did.

I can't remember every game we played/coached in that year… but I do remember this – we went undefeated the regular season like giving up only 20 something points all year. Then we moved through the playoffs – not getting scored on – and then we won the championship…. On a blocked punt to say the least!

But, looking back during that year – it was by far the most exciting time of my coaching career. One thing that really sucked was after the 93 season Coach Pruitt would move down to a lower level and me, Pablo and Tony would stay up. We just finished an undefeated season and kicked everyone's ass but we wouldn't be able to keep the thing going. Unfortunately the winning streak would end shortly thereafter because the Head Coach that took over the following year was a freaking idiot and the worst coach I've ever experienced in my life. But that's another story…

Tony and I would go on to continue coaching several more years, and he soon would take over a head coaching job for another team. I ran the defense and he switched to offense so now he'd bug me the same as Pablo and Larry. We were successful in a making playoffs and championships but not the dominance we shared the 93 season. We coached a few years at Santa Teresa…our goal was to make sure the kids understood what it took to play football, how to be a teammate, how to sacrifice, blood, sweat and tears… I have one story I will talk about in a bit – but back to the regular scheduled programming!!!

The kids on our Berryessa team were a rag tag bunch. There were kids on that team that I used to say "I would never want to meet in an alley"…. And I meant that… Tony and I were the only 2 white dudes on the entire team, so it was a culture shock to say the least, but it was absolutely AMAZING! I was the DB coach, my job was to make sure NOBODY got deep on us or went around us in a sweep….I can honestly say, the DB's I had my first year of coaching made it easy for me – Bermudez and Martinez at corner – they hit like tanks and were as fast as lightning. Dukes and Rivera were the Safeties and were experienced and savvy. They always seem to be in the right place at the right time. The best thing about this group is they were like sponges – they wanted to learn and they did.

That defensive back unit was dominate and we'd even bring in subs who would contribute. In fact, I can honestly say, we shut-down every passing team there was – including the mighty Milpitas team who loved to line up 3-4 receivers to one side every down. If they passed we'd smack the receiver, break up the pass or intercept it. My DB's were amazing…. And the cool thing is, they went on to become amazing football players in high school.

During the games, my only thing was keeping Lombardi cool during a game. Constantly tugging at him telling him to "get back"!!!!! HA! But he and I were in sync, we knew what we both were going to call before we even did it. There would be times I tell him to call a certain blitz and boom we did it, and it worked, like every time. That defense was the most impressive I have ever seen at that level or even in high school level. I think Ken honestly didn't have to worry about the defense, he saw that we had it in control. But he'd grind on Lombardi from time to time just to keep him in check because that little dude was just cocky as shit. I love it!!!

When we won the championship, it was one of the most amazing feelings I ever had. Seeing those kids work so hard and be so successful! They were a very

very talented bunch to say the least. I still remember being at the PAL stadium…. And taking our team picture with the championship banner…. It was one of the most amazing feelings I ever had. I got to see those kids work their butts off and be successful.

Having my first year coaching experience being part of that team was a life changing event for me. I was dealing with a difficult time in my life but I was able to spend time doing something I loved and make some great memories to last me a lifetime. Not to mention develop some great friendships along the way. Tony and I became almost like brothers. I had to constantly look after that little shit, but hey that's what brothers do. Till this day we remain close. Even though I've lost hair I'm still better looking and well Tony, he's gotten a little wider but our love for football and each other will never go away. But looking back, none of this would have occurred had I not opened the newspaper that one fateful day.

Chapter 10
The Buckhorn

The Pruitt's grew up in Compton during the 60's so I'm sure they were very active in the culture and given their personality, were active in their community and I'm sure they probably got into many scuffles with the police and authorities. Honestly, I think they may have been involved in a group named after a specific big black cat. Coach Pruitt would have been the leader and Ricky the enforcer....umm I mean advisor.

We used to go the pizza parlor after games, very common in coaching. This is when Darrel would show me the art of drinking Ice T from Long Island or the famous combo of Jack Daniels and Coke. Next door to the pizza parlor was a bar called "The Buckhorn". One night I noticed the Pruitt's weren't in the pizza parlor. I asked Coach Pablo where they were. He responded "at the Buckhorn, but you can't go over there". Well, being cocky and naïve, of course I didn't care. I just wanted to hang with my mentors. With my wingman, Coach Darrel and I walked over to the bar.

We get to the bar, opened the door and I swear it was just like the movie "Weird Science" when the two white boys Gary and Wyatt walked into the all black bar. The smoke filled the room all of the sudden fell silent and all the brothers in the bar just turned and starred at us. Half the room starred at us like "who the hell these white boys, they must be out of their damn mind", and the other half looked like "we got some white boys in here, and they ain't leaving."

Darrell and I just froze and looked at each other like "what the hell did we just walk into." We saw the Pruitt's sitting at the back table with what seemed like 7 or 8 other guys. Coach Ricky was sitting with his back against the wall. He leaned back in his chair and with his stone cold eyes, shook his head like we just messed up. Coach Pruitt, the leader he is, got up from the table and gave a nod to the room and walked over to us. He came up to us and with a sly smile and wonderment asked "you guys lost, what are you guys doing in here". He told the bartender the drink was on him and he then told us to keep our mouth shut, have the drink and go back to the pizza parlor. The bartender, chuckled while shaking his head and poured us the drink. I can't tell you what the drink was but I can tell you that was the fastest drink we had in our life.

Later that night, the Pruitt's came back to the pizza parlor and they were laughing telling the story to the other coaches. Coach Larry Lee joked "we're lucky they let us walk out alive" and Coach Pablo always one to laugh, looked at us and said he warned us and bet we won't do that again. Before the evening ended, Coach Pruitt looked at me and Darrel with a serious look and simply said, "Don't ever go over there without me."

Later on that season we were celebrating another victory and shutout. By this time it was a tradition; we dominated and just beat the shit out of some team and we would go celebrate at the pizza parlor. And at some point Ricky would disappear and soon after Coach Pruitt would follow. I swear we didn't know why, they served the same drinks at the pizza parlor but the Buckhorn was their place. So we're partying and as usual Coach Pruitt stood up and said he's going over to the "Horn". But this time and for some reason, probably with alcohol courage, I asked Coach Pruitt if me and Darrel could tag along. He grinned and said "come on". Darrel was cooler but for me I felt like a kid going on a field trip with my mentor.

The door opened and just like before the room turned silent and everyone looked at who was entering their domain. Coach Pruitt stood with me and Darrel practically holding on either side of him. He didn't say a word, just strolled in as only he could and started over to the table at the back where the group was. Coach Ricky was sitting in his usual spot, and just like before leaned back in his chair but this time he grinned and nodded his head with approval like we've been accepted.

That night I felt like we were one of the boys, we were part of the group. Laughing, swearing, telling jokes, talking trash and of course a lot of drinking. By the end of the night, the two white boys had entered their domain and were most likely hanging with a group of black cats. We were accepted part of the group and had a great time but most importantly, we successfully left. Needless to say, we never entered again…

Chapter 11
The Players

Similar to the movie "Sandlot", what made this group of players so special and unique is they all pretty much lived on the same streets or in the same neighborhood. As well, they had all been playing together for the Berryessa Cougars since they were 6 or 7 years old. Even other players joined us that season but they were either cousins or friends of our current players.

Growing up in East San Jose is not an easy thing. We had such a diverse group of players from ethnicity, income level and familial backgrounds. Some kids would live in a 1 bedroom apartment with a single mom that wouldn't be home because she was working 2 or 3 jobs and they would have to take care of there of younger brother or sister. Other players would go home to family of four with both parents to a house up in the hills. Even though they had different backgrounds, the common bond they shared is they still grew up in a tough area of San Jose, went to the same schools and surrounded by a team of players that weren't afraid of anyone.

By no means is my plan to disrespect any player that wore the maroon and gold uniform. In-fact, if I wanted to write an additional 100 pages it would be easy to talk about all the members of that team. But in the interest of simplicity I'll share on only a few players.

(#33) JOHN NORTH // PLAYMAKER

Now if there was a weakness to Coach Pruitt, it was his play calling on offense. Which to put it mildly was average at best. Even though I revere and love Coach Pruitt, if you asked players they would most likely agree that the 93 team was built around the defense. But what did make our offense go was this naturally gifted running back that looked as smooth as Marcus Allen. He had deceptive speed with his long strides and he glided when he had the ball in hands. Unfortunately he would only have the ball in hands like 8 or 9 times a game. But offensively he was our best player and when the game was on the line Coach Pruitt at least new who to give the ball to.

(#7) STEVEN MEDINA // LEADER

Quarterback was another weakness which probably explained Pruitt's hesitation to pass the ball. However, for the Reno Bowl game, we recruited a new player to join our team on the trip, Steven Medina. He came to us from our arch rival, Coyote Creek, this only added more to the rivalry. Medina brought a calmness and leadership ability to our offense as well as our team. He was basically Coach Pruitt on the field. He wouldn't get rattled and when it came time to make plays, he did.

(#58) BRANDON LATTIMORE // LOT-A-HEAD

As I mentioned earlier, part of the byproduct to coaching is the relationships you build with the players beyond the football field. Brandon Lattimore and I would continue our coach player relationship, he would later join my staff and we became really good friends later in life.

Similar to coaches getting nicknames, it's not uncommon for players to get nicknames from coaches. To give a physical description of Lattimore, he was a little bodied player with a huge oversized head, kind of like a Pez candy dispenser. So naturally his nickname for me became "Lot-a-head".

Even though he had a funny nickname he was one of those players that would never leave my side. He wasn't one of the bigger players and he ran funny. But the one thing you he did have you can't coach, he had a knack for making big plays. He started at outside linebacker but he also would usually be subbed out when we went to a cover 2 (2 safety's). I never had to look or yell for him because throughout the game he literally would be right behind me. And for what seemed like after every play he would say "Coach let me go in", "I can make the play" or something like that. I'd be lying if I didn't give him credit. Anytime we intercepted a pass, created or recovered a fumble, Lot-a-head was sure to be involved.

(#34) CHARLES HOBBS // BAD ASS

If there was ever a player that gave us an edge, attitude and toughness it was Charles Hobbs. He was a cousin of Ronald Moffitt (who started at the other outside linebacker). Hobbs was a kid that I swear was as grizzled and tough as a 25 year old man living in the hood. In fact, Coach Darrel and I would have to flip a coin as to who was going to driving him home after practices. To put it mildly he lived in the projects, the roughest part of town. Thankfully I won the coin flip and Coach Darrel had to drive him home first. And as you remember, we are both white.

Darrel tells the story…"Dude, you're gonna shit your pants when you take Hobbs home. I'm driving him home and then I pull on this street and there's cars everywhere and a bunch of guys just standing along the street or on the balcony's. As I'm driving they are just staring at me and all I'm trying to do is keep my head straight and not look around. As I pull up to this building, Hobbs looks at me and tells me to not get out of the car and don't turn around to leave, just drive straight. This advice is coming from a 14 year old who honestly was tougher than us and if something went down he'd be the first one to protect us.

He was the final piece that put the perfect storm together. Even though all the players on the team weren't afraid and wouldn't back down, we had the one guy who wasn't afraid to take it to the next level and drive fear into the opponents. He'd talk shit, instigate and intimidate. He was the enforcer and protector that every championship team at any level needs. Think Ronnie Lott, Lawrence Taylor and Charles Hayley etc…simply put, the other team knew not to mess with Hobbs.

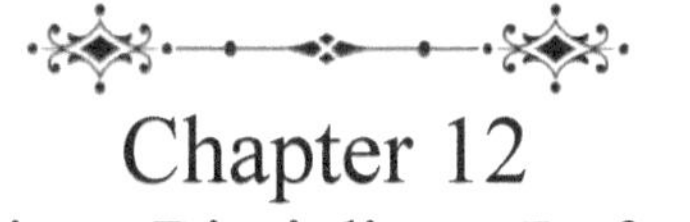

Chapter 12
Desire…Discipline…Defense

To win a championship, teams have to be sound in all aspects of the game. Blocking, tackling, offense, defense and special teams. Having athletes helps and as Coach Pruitt would tell us at meetings "Players win games but Coaches win Championships." Again, another bit of wisdom my mentor would drop on me. But if you were to ask the players, coaches as well as the opposing teams, the 93 Berressa Cougars were led by one of the nastiest defenses the league has ever seen before and even after that season.

The offense, led by the leadership and timely passing of Medina and the playmaking ability of North provided solid and consistent play. Similar as the character of Coach Pruitt, they were consistent, steady, and methodical and hate to say it, maybe a little boring….but it worked. The defense forced the other team to make mistakes and Pruitt's offense would get the ball and just move down the field to score. It's not fair to say they were boring, Medina was the perfect field general and North the perfect breakaway back complimented by shifty Rivera, powerful Hobbs and a couple playmaking receivers in Dukes and Bermudez. They put plenty of pressure on the other team's defense.

They were the complete contrast of our defense. We were aggressive, intimidating and definitely not boring. It was like watching Barry Sanders with the ball in his hands or Michael Jordan, you were glued to them because you anticipated seeing something special. It was like every snap we expected something to happen and more times than not, something usually did.

Big hits on a running back in the backfield, sacking the quarter back and blowing up the wide receiver if he dared catching the ball. Having almost 5 or 6 guys on every tackle were just every down occurrences. But it became routine to expect either a big hit, a fumble, interception or sack on every play. And of course, at the end of every play you could hear our player's high fiving, laughing, smiling, barking (literally) or pointing to the other team. Now I'm not going say I encouraged this, but it's kind of hard for the players to not carry this attitude when they'd hear myself, Coach Darrel and even Pablo talking shit to our own offense and other coaches. Practices became like games to us and sometimes Pruitt would have to yell at us to calm us down.

By no means can I take the only credit for the defense. It was a blending of all the coaches and the players along with a serious "F - You" attitude. It was the philosophy, the coaches, the players and whole lot of arrogance. It was if we all had a big chip going into this season. Me personally, being a skinny (at that time) and short white guy I always walked with a big chip and felt like I always had something to prove. My buddies would always say I have a Napoleon complex, which is to say I was a short little guy that always had to be in charge. When Darrel joined the staff we went to another level. Not only was he a great addition coaching wise, he and I shared the same mentality with how we viewed defense. This combined with the type of players we had only developed into the perfect storm.

When the preseason opens, teams spend time scrimmaging and practicing against each other. At this time, we really didn't know what we had and we didn't have a personality yet. However, when we first got the chance to line up against an offense that didn't wear our same uniforms, things changed pretty quickly. You could see the thunder clouds forming and the lightning in the distance. There was a storm brewing, we could see it, hear it but not sure when it would come. Well, it didn't take long…

Chapter 13
Sweet Revenge

After a few weeks of knocking heads with each other we were finally able to get to scrimmage against another team. As luck would turn out, the team that knocked us out of the playoffs last season will be our first team to play against, EYAC. It wouldn't be a stretch to say that we didn't look at this a just another practice or scrimmage. After they knocked us out of the playoffs last year, (because of the Coach Dave), we couldn't wait to scrimmage and to let them know just how much we felt about them.

We were a confident team….a more aggressive team…a get in your face team….simply, a better team. So as I mentioned, the perfect storm didn't take long to get going. And just like the previous year, EYAC's first offensive play they tried to throw a pass. Only this time the QB was pressured and threw a rushed passed. And of course Lattimore picked it off and scrambled in for a defensive touchdown. What we thought we could be on defense was perfectly captured on the very first play. And just like that….the storm just started.

Now of course 1 play doesn't define a practice, scrimmage or a game, but this particular play illustrated what would become the hallmark of our defense. Aggressive, constant pressure and big plays.

Needless to say we would go on and score 2 more touchdowns, have numerous sacks, and turnovers. And of course after every big hit, sack and turnover the players wanted to be sure and remind EYAC that we aren't the same team they played last year. When all of the carnage was done after that scrimmage, we successfully left our mark and righted a wrong from the previous year. We destroyed them 70 – 0. Message sent.

I remember after the scrimmage when I was standing next to Coach Pruitt and he was talking to the EYAC head coach. I overheard when their coach said "your defense is nasty, you guys are gonna be handful this year." Even he knew a storm was brewing in the forecast for that season.

Chapter 14
Season Starts...Storm Begins

Being my first year as a coordinator I loved taking stats. I believed in the philosophy that numbers don't lie. So I was big in keeping stats and taking notes throughout the season. When I found these notes in my memory box it only brought the moments of this season even more memorable.

WEEK 1 – WILLOW GLEN RAMS

I'll just some up and say we started the season by introducing ourselves to the rest of the league by pitching a shutout, which you'll find out became a theme for us. But we didn't just keep them from scoring, we punished the QB with 4 sacks, forced 4 turnovers and returned an interception return for touchdown.

Win 33 – 0   (1 – 0)

WEEK 2 – COYOTE CREEK

We cannot talk about the 1993 Berryessa Cougars without giving respect to our nemesis and arch rival, Coyote Creek. They were the team we circled on our calendar because we wanted to kick their ass more than any other team. And for them, the feeling was mutual. They were only in the league three or four years. But they were started by former Coaches and Parents from the Berryessa family. I'm not sure of the details but I believe many of those Coaches and Parents were friends of Coach Pruitt. I believe they wanted Pruitt to come with them and lead them in building the program from the ground up. He declined and after they left they started talking trash about him so I'd imagine the relationships soured. When they left our organization and formed their own teams, of course they naturally stole players from within our boundaries. So along with the Coach Pruitt thing, this created a new rivalry which didn't take long to get heated.

Leading up to "Creek Week", Coach Pablo came up with that, I knew there was something more about this game. Even the usual stoic and calm demeanor Coach Pruitt was a little more intense for these guys. He didn't really curse that much, I think Coach Darrel and myself did that enough for all the coaches, but for Coyote Creek he would let it be known that he wanted us to "kick their ass". So naturally, this gave me and Darrel even more motivation. It didn't take much to get me going anyway, but now it was like pouring gasoline on a blazing inferno because my head coach, teacher and mentor was locked in, and I had to have his back.

Coyote Creek players by no means were soft. If anyone had the same self-confidence and swagger it would be them. They had big, fast and talented players who loved to trash talk as much as we did. So naturally this game was right down our alley. To give this game the type of significance for the players would be like comparing Florida St vs. Miami back in the early 90's. These players grew up on the same streets and they either would play against one another in high school or become team mates. To give an example of the talent from both teams. Every year, the Bay Area would have a High School All-Star game for the graduating seniors. There are roughly over 4,000 players to choose from and only 80 are invited to play. In the 1998 All Star Game, there were 5 players who either wore Maroon and Gold for the Berryessa Cougars or Silver and Red from the Coyote Creek Wildcats from the 1993 season.

This was early in the season and only our second game. We had just smacked Willow Glen 33 – 0 the week before and now we are getting ready to play our rival at their home. We usually arrive a couple hours before our game and meet in the stands. Walking to the stadium and passing people wearing Red and Silver shirts or hats, I could feel their stares. I loved walking in wearing my colors. I wanted everyone to know where I'm from and who my team is. The more stares and comments I heard the more I relished it. In case you forgot, it doesn't take much to get me going and playing in another opponent's field and especially if it's hostile, I can't get enough of it.

I was new to this rivalry and honestly had no history to draw from it. But if I felt this way, I guarantee you the other coaches and players felt the same if not more. When we all went to the locker room we walked past their team. Even though Creek just lost the week before, you can just tell they were locked in and couldn't wait to get after it. There coaches were mean mugging us and talking a little trash. I couldn't wait to get after it. Having smacked EYAC in the preseason and dominated Willow Glen I had all the confidence the defense was going to be on point.

We left the locker room and began our walk to the field. With our players walking hand-in-hand the fans from Coyote Creek would make a path for us. I can remember hearing comments like "not today" or "bout to get a beat down". And those probably came from the 80 year old grandma's. After all the things leading up to the game, we're finally able to kick the ball off and get after it.

This was only my 3rd game as coordinator with a defensive playbook that I designed. I remember drawing X's and 0's and making alignments and scheming blitzes all Summer long and creating what would be known as the "Lombardi Defense". It would be safe to say, I actually didn't really know what I was doing and was just barely older then the guys I'm signaling plays to. When I created the playbook I used all kinds of different formations and looks. I thought it looked good and also made me feel like I had a little bit of knowledge. Needless to say, when things get pressured you'll find the cracks pretty quickly. Well in this game, the cracks became craters.

As you'd expect in a rivalry game, it was going to get heated and physical. Coyote Creek isn't Willow Glen. These guys were not going to just let us impose our will on them. Quite contrary, they actually imposed their will on us, or shall I say me. They had two playmakers that anytime they carried the ball they were a load to bring down, #44 and #5. #44 was a bruising back and it seemed like every time they gave him the ball he was dragging our players behind him. And when #5 got the ball he was breaking away from our players.

It didn't matter what I called, 44 Stack, 53 Monster, 52 Pinch etc…etc…etc...we simply couldn't stop either one of their running backs. They ran our ass up and down the field. I remember it was in the late in the 3rd quarter and Coyote Creek had the ball and they were on the move again. Coach Ricky came to me on the sidelines and asked me "What the hell am I doing" and I said "I'm trying everything, I can't stop them." He looked at me with the familiar stare I've been accustomed to know and said "You can't stop them?" And I had to admit that I was outmatched and said "I don't know what else to do."

So of course, Coyote Creek would go on and score again. We are now down 20 – 14 with a little less than 4 minutes to go in the game and the offense gets the ball. I'm frazzled and putting all my hope that Coach Pruitt will lead the offense to get another touchdown and we can squeak out a win. I felt helpless, defeated and yes I did question my abilities.

Medina leads the offense on a drive and we get the ball to midfield. There is now a little less than 2 minutes to go in the game and Coach Pruitt makes the perfect play call. Medina drops back to pass and completes it to North over the middle who makes a couple of moves and takes it to the house….we tie the game at 20. We kick the all-important extra point (which is 2 in our league) and we are now leading 22 – 20.

Damn it….we have to go back on defense with about a minute left and I haven't been able to stop them. I finally learned something during this game. Sometimes it's not about how many plays you have, but how well you play the ones you have. So instead of calling all kinds of things I made it simple. I didn't want to do anything crazy, just make sure the guys keep the ball in front of them and "everyone" get to the tackle. Well it worked….we pulled off the win. This was a true test of what kind of team we really had. Because even though I thought the defense was the best part of our team, for us to come back and depend on the offense when the defense sucked, proved that this team was destined for something special.

Win 22 – 20 (2 – 0)

Chapter 15
Lombardi Defense…2.0

Well after the scare from Coyote Creek, needless to say I had to rethink how we do things on defense. We knew we had way too much talent to give up as many points as we did. And to be honest, I took it as a personal attack on my coaching ability and felt like I have something to prove. Not just to myself, but to the players, the other coaches but especially to Coach Pruitt for entrusting me to be in this position. I knew I had to get better and was fully committed to do whatever needed to be done to make sure we are not in that position again.

So that night celebrating at the pizza parlor, there wasn't too much joy between me and Darrel. I'd include Coach Pablo and Larry Lee but they always had joy and had way too much fun. The outcome didn't really faze them, we won, and they've been coaching too long to get caught up and not enjoy themselves. But this was different for me and Darrel. He was my wingman and he knew I was pissed. Here we should be feeling good about a great game we were just in, but instead we were already talking about what we needed to do differently. Of course we always want to do our best and win games but in reality the one thing Darrel and I were focused on was being perfect, this is how we thought…..all the time.

We wanted the defense to be perfect on every play in every game. No excuses.

So as we started to talk, draw plays, evaluate our players and we came to one conclusion that would become a motto throughout our coaching career. We needed to simplify so the players can just act on instinct instead of "thinking". When a player "thinks" on a football field they are slow to react because they are not acting on instinct. In the game of football, if a player reacts a half second too late, a simple play can turn into an 80 touchdown.

To give an example. When you first learn to ride a bicycle at 4 years old you'll fall and crash because it's something new and you're thinking about peddling, steering and not falling. But when you ride a bike again 30 years later those thoughts don't enter your mind because you're just acting on instinct, riding a bike became natural to you. We wanted the same thing on our defense. We want guys playing fast and flying around so they will make plays.

We had incredible athletes and we just wanted to rearrange them a little different and allow them to use their athletic ability. We decided to move Hobbs (our bad ass) right up front because then all he had to do was just beat the guy in front of him and find the ball and because we wanted Hobbs to be the first guy the quarterback would see when he was trying to hike the ball. We also decided to only use the 5 man front and let the linebackers just read and react to the ball. We had these 2 stud corner backs, Bermudez and Martinez so we said let's just let them take away the outside receivers and we won't worry about them. This way we can use the other 9 players to focus up front. We did a little tweaking with our blitzes and coverages and then we had it. The new and improved "Lombardi Defense 2.0".

Chapter 16
Season Continues

So now that we've had a week to practice and prepare with our updated defense it was time to see if me and Darrel's 2.0 Defense will work. All week leading up the game all the coaches and players took it personal that we were pushed to the brink of defeat. But more importantly we actually looked vulnerable and beatable. That week in practice we were lighting up the offense and were bringing it. After making the adjustments in practice we couldn't wait to play the game.

WEEK 3 – CAMBELL-SARATOGA RAIDERS

Well to put it mildly, it was really unfortunate that the Campbell-Saratoga Raiders were our next opponent. But in all honesty, it didn't really matter, it was going to be a blood bath no matter who it was we played. We were flying all over the field and just as we wanted to do, the players were even faster and more aggressive than before. And of course this led to even more arrogance and cockiness so we picked up a couple of penalties, but Coach Pruitt was probably ok with it. We recaptured what we had against EYAC and Willow Glen and we even improved and made our defense even more menacing. Needless to say, we killed them. We had 6 sacks, 2 Interceptions, 3 fumbles and 1 touchdown. It wasn't even close and it was just like it was supposed to be.

WIN 35 – 0 (3 – 0)

WEEK 4 – NABATO YARO

If there was a team whose players were rougher and more intimidating than our players was the team called Nabato Yaro. The name doesn't necessarily mean anything, it was more of the location that these players lived in, East Palo Alto. EPA, as we called them, was literally the ghetto. To give the best description, it's basically Compton of the Bay Area. Every weekend there seemed to be shootings, car thefts and robberies. Hobbs lived in a rough area in San Jose, but East Palo Alto made Hobbs area look like a vacation spot.

The unfortunate thing about Nabato Yaro is they pretty much had to forfeit almost every game. They never had enough players to play or the players they had couldn't make the legal weight. The morning of the game, Darrel and I rode together, primarily because we thought it would be better to take his truck because it would be less tempting to steal. Not to mention, we're kind of scared shitless because again, we're the only 2 white guys on the team, so we thought strength in numbers. We pull into the school parking lot, and it was littered with trash, broken bottles and broken down cars missing wheels or smashed in windows. And this was the "school" parking lot. We tried to find the closest parking spot and immediately Darrel and I get into the locker room and look for Coach Ricky. We just thought it would be best to stick by his side, pretty much the entire day. Yeah you could say we're chicken shit, but we were way out of our element.

We made our adjustment last week and we're back to kicking ass. But this was a different kind of team that we are about to play. Even though we had this aura around us and building a reputation that we were going to bring it not just by winning, but by physically dominating and imposing our will. Nabato Yaro had a different kind of reputation.

Everyone in the league new Nabato Yaro was a physically superior and nasty team. But they played undisciplined so if you could withstand the penalties, cheap shots and dirty plays, you'd most likely win the game. When they did have the ability to play a game, they spent most of the time not trying to win the game, but wanted to literally fight on almost every play. Even their coaches and parents in the stands talked shit and even encouraged them to fight. That team was straight crazy and it was even more insane when they had a home game. You talk about home field advantage, they had it simply because the environment was nothing like any other team in our league played in. Playing a game at their house was not about just winning, it was more like trying to survive and get the hell out of there….assuming you still had your car.

In our league, players had to make a certain weight so as to make the teams similar and be fair competitively. This way neither team has a physical advantage by simply having bigger players. In the locker room with their team were some guys in high school and as predicted they didn't have enough players to field a team.

Here we'd driven an hour to come play a game and it looked like we weren't going to be able to play because they would have to forfeit. As I mentioned, by this time we had a swagger about us. We had the attitude like the Miami Hurricanes, the U. We were brash and arrogant and instead of apologizing when we smacked the shit out of our opponents, we'd point and laugh in their face. We knew we were better than anyone and we knew they knew that. We walked, talked and played like we were the shit…simply because we were.

Nabato Yaro knew what kind of reputation we had and obviously by no means did we intimidate these guys. They wanted a piece of us so bad and for them to have to forfeit made all their coaches and players pissed off. If there was a team to challenge them in toughness, physical intimidation and above all, cockiness and swagger, was us. They knew it, and they also knew we knew it. We weren't afraid (aside from me and Darrel) and our players are wanting to test themselves also in this environment.

Both teams are in the locker room and our players hear Nabato Yaro will have to forfeit. Without hesitation, Hobbs spoke up "f@%# that, let them all play" and then we could hear Lattimore say "We gonna win anyway". Even though they technically didn't have enough "legal players" after Hobbs and Lattimore said that, everyone with Nabato Yaro (including the high school guys) and even older guys said, "we all playing now." At this time, Coach Pruitt could have taken the easy win by forfeit, but since we did allow everyone to play (even the guys not on their roster) the game became official.

We are warming up before the game and tension is at an all-time high. Coach Ricky was on high alert and ready to beat some heads even more so than usual. So as the players go thru the routine, typically they would finish up and go to the end zone for our Unity Prayer. This time, instead of going to our end zone, the team went to our sidelines and got into formation. At this point I should inform you that "after" our games the players would jog the track as a celebratory victory lap. We did this to build team unity and feel good about ourselves, but mostly we did it to gloat and rub in the face of the team we just smacked. While they jogged they would chant "We are BC" or "We are Maroon and Gold" etc…

But this time, BEFORE the game and of course led by Hobbs, the team started to jog the track for their "Victory Lap". This kind of stuff doesn't happen before games because generally there is an unwritten rule of respecting the other team's side lines. However, this game was already different because of what happened in the locker room. Our team is jogging and doing the usual chants, but then as they get close to the Nabato Yaro stands they slow down. Then all of the sudden they started chanting "Who Don't Want None" and then pointing to the crowd and the sidelines saying "They Don't Want None". They didn't just do this once….they kept repeating the chant and pointing every time.

None of us coaches knew anything about this because the players made it up on the fly. We're like "what the hell are they doing, they are about to start a riot". But this was our team; brash, arrogant and didn't back down from anyone. Needless to say the players and coaches on their sideline are going nuts and the fans are beyond pissed, yelling and even throwing stuff at them as they jog past them. Of course this didn't stop them, it only made our guys get louder and more emphatic with saying "They Don't Want None". They were marking their territory, they even jogged through the cheerleaders who were on the track. It was a scene.

After their jog, I met them in the end zone for the Unity Prayer. As I mentioned this was our war cry and when we'd finish with "Kick Some Ass" it always hyped us up. But this time, it wasn't about being hyped up. We were already there at the highest level we could be. I swear this time the Unity Prayer was the loudest I've ever heard. The player's eyes were glazed over in a different look. They starred as if they were a pack of lions getting ready to hunt its prey. It wasn't about playing a football game now. It was about sending a message that we didn't give a shit who we played and where we played. We knew we were the big dogs anytime we stepped on the field. And on that day, on Nabato Yaro's home field, to end our Unity Prayer with the epic "Kick Some Ass", it was beyond loud, it was deafening it was as if a pack of lions roared.

Nabato Yaro was getting ready to kick the ball off and Coach Pruitt was looking at one of the Nabato Yaro players and said "That guy has a beard…what the hell did we just do?" Not only did they have bigger players and high school players on the team, but they even suited up grown ass men.

After our scare against Coyote Creek and getting our swagger back against Campbell-Saratoga we just knew that all we had to do was play our steady game on offense and turn our defense loose and we would be fine. Regardless of where we are playing and even who we are playing, we just need to be us. Once the ball was kicked, it was game on and we knew we were going to put another spanking on just another team.

Even with the craziness before the game, Nabato Yaro, played undisciplined and when they figured out that we were just as big a bullies as they were and they eventually got frustrated. We weren't intimated, didn't back down and matched them with physical play, they eventually made mistakes and ultimately broke. North would break long TD runs and Medina would make timely passes. The defense continued our dominance and had 4 sacks, 4 turnovers and yes, we scored another touchdown. And of course, we had to let them know after every big play that it didn't matter where or who we played, we were the bad asses whenever we stepped on the field.

However, after we beat them up, this time Coach Pruitt told the players we're not doing the victory lap, we just need to get the heck out of there while we still can.

Win 33 – 0   (4 – 0)

WEEK 5 – EVERGREEN KODIAKS

Evergreen is always a well-coached team that have good athletes. We have a lot of respect for this team because they always seem to hang in games and win more than they lose. It could be because we just came off an emotional win at Nabato Yaro the week before but the game was closer than expected. Unfortunately our defensive touchdown streak ended and nothing special happened in this game except we took our winning streak to 5.
Win 13 – 0   (5 – 0)

WEEK 6 – UNION CITY COLTS

This was one of my favorite games all season. It was rainy, muddy and we were all slipping and sliding all game. I remember the field was a mess, especially the sidelines. I have a habit of getting excited when big plays happen and I'll start running down our sidelines. Well on this day it seemed like I fell on my ass like 3 times. All I know is after the game, I was just as muddy as the players.

Union City is a team of athletes that seems to compete for championships every year.   They typically have a few legit players that will go on to star in high school and even get college scholarships. Well this team was no different. They had a few stud players, but especially the running back, Adams. I love North, he was smooth and glided with the ball in his hands. But Adams ran like Eric Dickerson when he got the ball in his hands. He was big, fast and could pound inside as well as break it long on any play. By far, he was the best back in our league.

Having learned from the Coyote Creek game we started to get better with game planning and calling plays. We figured out that our front 3 guys continuously brought pressure right up the middle and our defense ends brought pressure from the outside. We basically collapsed the whole offensive front and suffocated the offense. Teams had a difficult time running the ball and when the running back carried the ball he was getting smacked by 3 or 4 guys every play. When teams tried to pass we were even more of a nightmare. Darrel and I got really good at calling blitzes at the right time and when the other team did try to pass it was usually a big play for us and it didn't really turnout to well for the quarterback. Our game plan was simple…key on Adams, get 3 or 4 guys in on ever tackle and the rest will fall in place.

It was early in the game, I believe the 2nd quarter. Adams got the ball and he was running towards our sidelines. I can see Martinez closing in and Moffitt, Riley and Hobbs tracking him down. It was one of those plays that seem to be in slow motion and you can see what was about to happen.

The play is coming towards our sideline right in front of me and Darrel. Before Adams could get out of bounds you hear a loud "crack" and then all of the sudden you see Adams, Hobbs and Riley flying through the air in front of us going out of bounds. You could hear the crowd yell "oooohhhh" as they watched Adams, Hobbs and Riley splash down and go sliding thru the mud and all the way to our benches. It was an awesome football play and really cool to watch right before our eyes.

Riley and Hobbs jump up in celebration and our sidelines and crowd are going crazy. And of course

Hobbs being Hobbs, was sure to let Adams know who just lit his ass up. Now as a Coach I never want to see players get injured and I want to beat teams while playing at their best. But on that play, Adams got up slowed and had to be helped to his sidelines. It was great that nothing serious happened to him and he would go on and play the rest of the season. However, his game against us ended on that play. He didn't want to run the ball again. The play fired us up even more and then it was lights out the rest of the game. Even though it was mud fest, we still did what we do. Medina led. North broke long and the defense scored another touchdown….and later in the game we would also knock out their Quarterback.

Win 24 – 0   (6 – 0)

WEEK 7 – ALMADEN WARRIORS

Coming into this game there were only two undefeated teams. The Almaden Warriors were 5-0-1 and we are 6-0. Because they had not been defeated we give them our full attention. But also, Almaden came from the "other side of the tracks" the rich side. Their parents drove newer BMW's and Mercedes Benz and most of our parents rolled up in old beat up Nissan's and Honda's with dents and miss matched doors. Our boys new this, so of course they just needed to get a little more motivation. And nothing says more motivation than a bunch of rich kids from the South Side coming to our home field. Not to mention the winner of this game would be the Division Champions and get the top seed in the playoffs.

Almaden was good, actually really good. They had 2 really good running backs and a quality Quarterback so I can see why they were undefeated. We jumped up on them early by creating turnovers on defense and the offense scored 2 quick touchdowns in the first quarter. This pretty much was the blueprint for all of our games.

There is this saying I learned over my years of coaching, the perfect play at the perfect time. We had been playing our usual shutdown defense, but we weren't making our big plays. It was mid-way thru the 3rd Quarter and they had the ball in midfield. I called a line stunt with the Linebacker Blitz and we got caught. Almaden made the perfect play call, it was quick run right up the gap that the Linebacker would normally be. The running back broke for over 40 yards to inside our 5 yard line. We still made it tough on them but ultimately they would score on 4th down. So after 4 games and 2 halves we would finally give up another score.

You'd think our players were pissed that our streak was broken, I know I was. But Lattimore would later tell me that when the running back scored he was grunting, screaming and yelling trying to score. After he scored our players just laughed at him and said "he sounded like a little girl." This was our team, never miss an opportunity to make fun of our opponents, even when they did something good.

On our next possession we couldn't move the ball again. We were inside our own 20 so we had to punt. Well the snap went over North's head (our punter). The football bounced all the way back inside our end zone. North ran back and picked up the football. Fortunately he was able to run it out to the 5 yard line and they had just scored the last time they had the ball. We hadn't scored again since the 1st Quarter so we are only still only ahead 12 – 7 and they have ball up close to our end zone again threatening to take the lead. We just lost our shutout streak, now we're looking a potentially ending our undefeated streak.

No more laughing, we needed to lock it in. 1st Down, smack, they don't move the ball. 2nd Down, whack, they lose yards. 3rd Down, crack, no yards. Comes down to 4th down and they snap the ball, and the running back tries to go up the middle and he is met by a wall of our players and they drive him back….no yards…..no score…no score.

Even though we prevented them from scoring, Almaden has all the momentum at this point and we get the ball inside our own 10 yard line. It's in the 4th quarter and we are able to find our rhythm on offense and start moving the ball. We pick up a first down and continue moving forward. Medina is being the general leading the offense, North is able to break off some runs and Dukes makes a couple of timely catches. We are moving the ball into their side of the field and more importantly taking time off the clock. We get the ball to their 40 yard line and then we hit the brakes. We can't move anymore. It's 4th down and we're not close enough to go for it so we need to punt the ball. There is a little less than 3 minutes left to go in the game and now we are going to give the ball back to Almaden and try to hold on to keep our undefeated season going.

The ball is snapped………and it goes over North's head AGAIN!!! The ball goes sailing back way over his head. So now he has to scramble back and picks it up at around our 25 yard line. He starts up the middle and then bounces it to the outside to their sidelines.

And just like the Adams play against Union City, you can see something happening in slow motion. As North starts to break up their sidelines he crosses the 50 he jukes inside and then bounces back outside and then all of the sudden it was like our players had the perfect picket fence. He runs past the 45….40 "crack" …35…30 "wham"….25….20 "smack" and he goes untouched down the sidelines and of course starts high stepping it into the end zone.

"DEFINITELY remember the Almaden game. That was one of my favorite games we played all year. That game was intense. I remember thinking the game was slipping away when that happened again. I couldn't believe the ball took a perfect bounce right back to me. After we scored it was incredible and everyone was going crazy. I think half the team on the sidelines ran to the end zone and celebrated with us. It was a surreal moment"…(John North)

"My favorite play that year. Ball snapped over John's head on the punt and we housed it down their sideline. It felt like the Indian run with everyone lined up. One block would get made and someone else would slide up and peel an Almaden player and then someone else would repeat."…(Brandon Lattimore)

Hysteria erupts on our side lines and in the stands. Coaches are jumping up and down and it seemed like all our players ran to the end zone to join in the celebration. Now just because these are 8th and 9th graders, they were well aware of the moment. When you start playing sports, the more you play and become more competitive, at some point you will cross the bridge to understanding the big moments in a game. And this, this was that moment and everyone knew it. Our players knew it, our fans knew it and even Almaden knew it. With that play we kept our undefeated season going and now we locked up the top seed going into the playoffs.

Win 20 – 7 (7 – 0)

WEEK 8 – MILPITAS KNIGHTS

After the Almaden game we get ready to close out the regular season against the Milpitas Knights. You would think that after such an emotional game we just played last week we would have a letdown, but not these guys, not this team. We cleared the final obstacle for the regular season and won our Division. But going into this game we didn't just have our eyes on winning the division, or keeping our winning streak alive. No, we wanted to get back on our shutout streak on defense. We took pride in our defense and we took it personal that we allowed another team to score.

Milpitas made the mistake of trying to pass on us so we put a beat down on their quarterback by sacking him 7 times, intercepted the ball twice, recovered a fumble and most importantly, got another shutout.

Win 24 – 0 (8 – 0)

Chapter 17
The Playoffs...Quest Begins

To us, the playoffs was just another part of the season to show our dominance. We really didn't fear anyone and knew we were destined to reach the Championship game. As expected we dominated our first two opponents and our over powering defense was on full display. In the first two rounds our defense actually scored a touchdown in both games and our offense would only score once in those two games.

PLAYOFFS ROUND 1 – WILLOW GLEN   Win 16 – 0 (9 – 0)

PLAYOFFS SEMIFINALS – EVERGREEN   Win 6 – 0 (10 – 0)

Chapter 18

Championship Game…the rematch

After the comeback win in Week 2 against Coyote Creek, we almost seemed destined to meet for the Championship. We knew they were the 2nd best team in the league and we actually wanted to play them again because we felt the first time we played them was a fluke. We dominated every other game except them and it just left a sour taste in our mouth. How could we be considered dominate if we had to comeback against an opponent and squeak out a win by 2pts?

Well as things would work out, the football Gods aligned the playoff bracket so the only way we could have a rematch would be if we met in the Championship game. Of course we knew we were going to be there. And I'm sure Coyote Creek felt the same way and wanted a rematch as badly as we did. Remember, even though this was a relatively new rivalry, it had all the makings of a bitter rivalry the same as between Michigan/Ohio State or Auburn/Alabama. Both teams have confidence, the athletes and all the swagger to get after it and settle it on the field.

Getting up for Creek Week was not hard to do, but now it was different….it was for the Championship. We got the rematch we wanted and frankly deserved. We knew that the only way to complete the perfect season was to beat not just the 2nd best team, but our rival. As a champion, you don't want to back into a victory or play a weaker opponent. To call yourself the "True" Champion, you need to beat the team that puts you to the test. You have to be on your game because they can match you physically, mentally and emotionally.

Coyote Creek was on a roll themselves. After they lost their first 4 games to start the season, they would win 6 in row to make the Championship game. Coyote Creek received the #6 seed and had a more difficult road to get to the game. They pulled the upset and beat Almaden in the first round and then rolled Milpitas in the semifinals. They were battle tested and have all the confidence. As expected, we continued our dominate streak through the playoffs and shut out Willow Glen and Evergreen. So of course, you know we had confidence.

"We felt like we were the better team. They beat us the first game by coming back and we were on a winning streak." (Israel, Coyote Creek player 93')

We needed to learn from our first game when #44 and #6 ran all over us the first time we played, and obviously I needed to be locked in and not scrambling like I was in that game. I had full confidence with the Lombardi Defense 2.0 and with me and Darrel's play calling. The players understood their roles and we had an energy of knowing and expecting things to happen. Because of our discipline and relentless pressure, at some point, we knew our opponent would break and make a mistake. And when they did, we would pounce on them like vultures on a fresh carcass.

As we learned in the first game, #44 and #5 were legit backs who could run fast and break tackles. The defensive game plan was simple…the linebackers; Riley, Moffett and Lattimore would key on #44 and #5 and the front five would bring the pressure right up the middle. Corners; Bermudez and Martinez would stay 1 on 1 with their wide receivers and we'd bring our safeties; Dukes and Rivera, closer up front to the line of scrimmage. In the first game #44 and #5 broke too many tackles so the most important thing is we have to get multiple guys to the ball carrier. We just needed to be ourselves on defense. Be physical, disciplined, get 4 or 5 guys on the tackle and punish whoever had the ball. Of course we'd do timely blitzes and just like all season long, make big plays...more on that to come.

Coyote Creek was no slouch on defense and they were physical as well. As I mentioned our offense was solid but not really explosive. We had the steady leadership of Medina at quarterback and we had our playmaker North, who should get the ball like every snap if possible. Our team was all about controlling the clock, managing on offense and waiting for the defense to create opportunities, which we did in every game up to this point.

The night before the championship game I had Hobbs, North, Lattimore and Moffett staying the night. We watched the game film from the first game against Coyote Creek and just talked about the game. We ate breakfast in the morning and this was a little bit different than any other time this season…nobody is saying a word. It's as if we all are focused and locked in on what is in front of us.

Driving to the stadium, playing my typical Phil Collins "In the Air of the Night" and still no one talks. We just listen and it seems like we've been in game mode all week long, but now it was only hours away. The locker room was quiet, not a nervous quiet, just seemed like the calm before the storm. We never really got nervous before games, we knew what to expect but now as a team, players and coaches, we're just completely focused on fulfilling our quest.

We're undefeated, it was Coyote Creek and it was the Championship Game. Everything we wanted from the first day of practice in July was right before us. We are playing the perfect opponent, in the perfect scenario, in search of the perfect season…again, it was the perfect storm. Everyone in the locker room knew it. In just about an hour, we were about to begin the completion of perfection.

At the stadium, the locker rooms are separated by the same wall. We're in the locker room and then we start to hear Coyote Creek players yelling and banging on the lockers. They were calling us out and talking trash from the other side of the wall. But it would get even more interesting before we even got to the field.

Both teams have their own entrances to the field, we head out of the locker room and we're standing on the path getting ready to start walking down. We hear this chanting with what sounds like "We are Creek" or something like that. Then all of the sudden the Coyote Creek players jog through our formation line. Here we are standing 2x2 holding hands and this team goes out of their way to walk around the building, break our line and jog down the middle of our players as they go to the field.

Now as you recall what we did before the game against Nabato Yaro. What we did was a "no-no" because of the unwritten rule of respecting your opponent. Well, this was at an all-time different level. Breaking the line of a team "while" they're standing in formation is beyond disrespectful. They weren't just trying to mark their territory, they were trying to tell us we ain't shit so they can do whatever they want.

Needless to say, we didn't need any more motivation. Here these punk asses want to disrespect us….Don't they know who we are? What we've done? And they want to call us out. Funny thing is, our players remained calm, even Hobbs. I could only imagine that this just made them even more focused on the task at hand. Coyote Creek didn't just poke the bear, they got a pack of Cougars ready to feast. It's about to go down.

Chapter 19
Championship Game...kick off

The game starts with Coyote getting the ball. And just as they did in our first game they started driving down the field. They picked up a couple of first downs and got all the way down inside our 30 yard line. The difference between this game and what happened in our earlier game, is this time I didn't panic. After the first time we played them, we have only allowed another team to score 7 points and had 8 shutouts up to this point. Even though they moved the ball, we ultimately stopped them and got the ball back to our offense.

As my coaching years increased and I gained more experience, I started to believe that what happens when a team first gets the ball it doesn't really matter because they have practiced their first 8 or 10 plays all week. I know this, because when I became a Head Coach, we would practice our first 10 plays as well. What I learned is, the game of football doesn't really happen in the first drive, it happens the next time they get the ball. That's when the adjustments are made. This is why I remember the words from Coach Pruitt, "Players win games, but Coaches win Championships." Championships are won by which team can make the best adjustments.

We didn't necessarily have to make much adjustments, we just needed to remind the defense of the game plan and just execute it. We knew that we only had to stop #44 and #6. They don't really pass so we can be ultra-aggressive, stay disciplined and get 4 or 5 guys in on every tackle. On their first possession they moved the ball down the field and gained a total of 33 yards on that drive. For the remainder of the first half they would only gain 10 more yards. Needless to say, the boys were locked in. It seemed like every time the announcer would call out who made the tackle, he would say 3 or 4 player's names.

I have to give credit to Coach Pruitt. Even though I made fun of his offense and called it boring, in this game he was really aggressive and called a great game. I know he wanted to win the championship because it's the championship but deep down I'm sure he wanted to kick Coyote Creeks ass just as bad. And especially after that stunt before the game, he wasn't the only one. I don't know if he was being aggressive because of what happened in the first game and he didn't trust me and the defense. Or that he was being aggressive *because* he trusted me and the defense.

The offense was moving the ball up and down the field and had twice as many yards as Coyote Creek. North and Rivera were breaking off 4 or 5 yards every time they carried the ball. Coach Pruitt called a reverse and Dukes picked up 30 yards. The only thing that kept the offense from scoring was themselves. In the first half we would fumble or make get a penalty that would kill our drive. We went to half-time tied.

The second half starts and we get the ball. Unfortunately for us Coyote Creek made some good adjustments so our offense stalled and we had to punt. When high stakes games are played and both teams are equally matched the difference in the outcome usually comes down to mistakes, most notably, turnovers. When we punted, the Coyote Creek player went to catch the ball and it bounced off his hands and we recovered the ball just 30 yards from their end zone.

We had a great opportunity. First down North picks up 7 or 8 yards, but then we can't pick up the first down and we had to give the ball back to Coyote Creek. Now they had the momentum, and of course on their first play #6 broke off a 15 yard run to get the ball near mid-field. Boom, just like that they turn the tables on us. But our adjustments still held up and the defense stopped them the next 3 plays and they had to punt the ball back to us.

Just like an intense tennis match, now was our turn for a big break. They punted the ball and it bounced over our players head. He went back and picked it up. He made a couple of jukes and down the sidelines he ran. The only person between him and the goal line was the punter who would make the tackle at their own 25 yard line. Again we were only 25 yards from scoring.

On first down, Coach Pruitt gave the ball to our playmaker North. He swung out to the right and cut back inside and picked up 13 big yards. We were almost inside their 10 yard line. You could feel the momentum shifting our way. We can hear the fans cheering us and our sidelines is amped up. Everyone was anticipating that we are going to score and get even closer to being crowned Champion. The very next play we snapped the ball...and we fumbled the ball, again.

I guess the best thing is Coyote Creek started their drive at their own 15 yard line so they had a long way to go. There was a little less than a minute left in the 3rd Quarter so we knew if the defense could stop them, we should get the ball back in good field position. Coyote Creek didn't help themselves, they would get called for penalties and the ball would move all the way back to their own 5 yard line.

The 3rd quarter ends and we switch sides. We stop them on both 2nd and 3rd downs and it was working out as we planned. It was 4th and very long so they were going to have to punt. I contemplated going for the block and see if we can score on defense. But then I remembered what happened a year ago with Coach Dave. The punter is standing inside the 5 yard line and we are just going to rush the front 3 players and set up the return to get good field position for the offense.

Coyote Creek snaps the ball and Fernandez destroys his blocker and rushes right up the middle. It just so happens that he was also one of the tallest players on our team. As he's closing in on the punter he sticks his hand up and blocks the punt. The ball is bouncing around and madness occurs. The ball bounces and one of our players scoop up the ball and runs into the end zone…..Touch Down!!! Honestly it couldn't have been a more perfect player to score the defensive touchdown. The one player that gave us the edge, toughness and swagger on defense…Charles Hobbs.

Obviously everyone is going crazy. We had been beating them up and down the field all night and had nothing on the score board to show for it. The entire season we had dominated and imposed our will on our opponents and just waited for them to make a mistake. And for our defense to score yet another touchdown in the Championship game…..it was simply poetic.

We kicked the ball back to Coyote Creek and they have about 7 minutes left in the game. Just like when sharks see blood in the water or lions have their sights set on their next prey, these Cougars were ready to go for the jugular. The one thing that teams hated to do against us was try to pass. Ultimately teams would have to because they were losing by so many points. But when teams did try to pass, we were like rabid dogs getting to the quarterback. When teams passed, this is when things would get really bad for them and quickly. We would either sack and cause a fumble or get an interception. When I saw Coyote Creek drop back to pass I knew we had them. The quarterback was forced out of the pocket and threw the ball in the air. Dukes jumped up and picked it off.

We got the ball back. Now all we had to do was keep running the ball, and take time off the clock and lock up our Undefeated Season. We snap the ball...and....fumble...again!!! So now all the momentum we just had with the block punt for touchdown and the interception swung right back to Coyote Creek. The only difference now is they have the ball at mid-field.

To my surprise they called another pass play but this time they completed it for 13 yards and picked up their only first down in the 2nd half. Now they seriously have the momentum. At this time I should tell you that we missed the extra point, so we only led 6 – 0. They have the ball near our 35 yard line and once more they drop back to pass. The quarterback is flushed out to the left again and he throws the ball to #6 who is wide open. The ball is in the air and somehow it gets tipped by one of our guys causing it to change direction. The ball goes behind #6 and Moffett reaches out and one handed tips the ball to himself for another interception and he runs back the other way. It was one of those plays you could just watch over and over again and still be impressed by the perfection of what had to happen on that play. Pressure, opportunity and big play.

We get all the momentum back and now there's a little more than 4 minutes left in the game. We have the ball at their 40 yard line and Coach Pruitt settled the offense down and emphatically told them to hold the ball with both hands. We just wanted to run the clock out. Well on this drive we successfully did move the ball and take precious time off the clock. Even though we didn't score on that drive, we gave the ball back to Coyote Creek with under a minute left in the game with 80 yards to go for a touchdown.

As I mentioned before, the 1993 team was known for toughness, aggressiveness, swagger and of course the defense. All told, when the game was under the brightest lights and with everything on the line, that defense stood up to let everyone know who they were.   For that game, on Coyote Creek's first possession they would get 33 yards, and for the rest of the game they would only gain 25 more yards. We would sack them once, get 2 interceptions, force a fumble and as faith would have it, score the winning touchdown in the Championship game.

Even though there was still time in the game, Coyote Creek's spirit was shattered and they knew the game was over and of course we knew the game was over. They were dejected, frustrated and simply just beat down. The game wasn't really that close except on the score board, and just like we had all season long we imposed our will and ultimately broke the spirit of our opponent.

We forced teams to make perfect blocks, perfect tackles, and to execute with perfection. For a team to beat us, or even compete with us, they needed to be perfect in every way. We knew that, and they knew that. But the only team that could be perfect the 1993 season, was us, and when the final horned sounded, we were.

Our boys rushed the field and every one euphoria hit. Not only was it a great game against our rival but we completed the perfect season and in spectacular fashion. Regardless of what level you play, or what sport you play, to go a whole season and to be undefeated is something special. Everyone that was a part of the team, starter or sub, should have fond memories because they were part of that team and they can forever call themselves a "Champion".

Coach Pruitt brings out the Championship banner and our boys get ready for one final victory lap. I guess they wanted to cherish it, and probably because they crushed Coyote Creeks spirits. But this time they didn't jog the track, they strolled. They strutted with the pride and swagger you'd only expect from that team. Doing the same chants and marking their territory.

Coach Pruitt is smiling from ear to ear and even Ricky has a grin. Pablo and Larry Lee are already getting ready to drink from their flask (inside Larry's jacket). Coach Darrel is jumping around like a little 4 year old girl. And me? Well the emotions are just too over whelming for me. I'm sitting on the bench and I'm just sobbing with joy, pure joy. Coach Pruitt, my mentor, the man that would see something in me that I didn't, looked over at me sitting by myself. With a huge smile, he would come over and give me a hug and tell me how proud he was of me. Looking back, I'm not sure what meant more, winning the championship or hearing those words from someone you revered. I guess both are just as meaningful.

Win 6 – 0   (11 – 0)

Chapter 20
The End....reflection

Maybe because I've officially hit the 50 number and I'm having what's called the mid-life crisis. Maybe it's because of the move from the place I've called home for basically my whole life. Maybe because I came across a bin marked "Football" and memories just overwhelmed me. I have no idea what prompted me to sit down at my laptop and just start typing whatever came to my mind.

A couple of my all-time favorite movies are "Stand By Me" and "Sandlot" and one of my favorite TV shows growing up was the "Wonder Years". I believe all of these have a similar theme and are stories about a reflection of a moment in time that a person feels had some significance in their life. I don't believe my story is about football. I believe it's more about the moments that occurred in my life that happen to coincide with the game of football.

There are many moments in time or seasons (in life or in sports) that happen in a person's life. If we sit back and allow ourselves to relive that moment later in life, we all may want to sit at a laptop. If we look back, we can all probably think of specific person, group or event that occurred in a moment and had such a profound effect on us that it impacted our life. Obviously meeting our spouses, having children, graduating and death of a loved one are all life changing events that we can recall. I meaning more of the moments that we just happened to come across by chance as if by design or on purpose. At the time, we may not realize the significance until later in life.

This usually occurs when we ask ourselves the inevitable "What if" questions that helps us ponder the path our life has taken. What if I drove home a different way and didn't see the practice? What if my brother didn't take the time to shoot pool with me on that day? What if Coach Darrel hadn't looked in the newspaper? What if Charles Hobbs, Steven Medina and others join our team? What if Coach Ricky didn't grill my ass on the sidelines? What if I never found the courage to speak up at half-time in the playoffs? What if Coach Pruitt didn't say "ok you got it"? What if, what if, what if. For the 1993 Berryessa Cougars, the "what if" started in 1992 at a bowl game in Reno. But for me the "what if" started that one fateful day when a little 6 year old girl would sit next to me on the bench.

So I guess I'm feeling nostalgic about a moment in my life that maybe only impacted me. I'm Kevin from Wonder Years, Gordie from Stand By Me or Smalls from Sandlot. The only difference, my story is not fiction, my moments of nostalgia are real….just like the players and coaches from that 1993 season are real.

It took me awhile, and some would say it still has never happened, but I finally matured and gained a little wisdom. I developed a saying that I would use later in life while teaching my high school students. "You need to go back to go forward". What I meant was we should take time to look back at our past. We can't go back in time and get stuck there, unfortunately that happens all too often to people. But rather we should take time to reflect on a moment from time to time that helps us learn about how we got to certain paths in our lives.

At what moment did we meet our spouse? (I walked into the wrong class in college and saw her, so I stayed) What moment did we meet our best friend? (We became roommates) What moment broke are heart? (When I carried my brother's casket)

I look back on that season and think of the coaches, the players and even the teams we played, especially Coyote Creek. Through victory or defeat we can only grow from our experiences. Just as in the birth of a newborn child or the passing of a loved one, the experience either way will have an effect on us. Those moments help us reflect and hopefully we learn about who we are and how we became the person we are today.

I'm an optimistic person because I generally believe only good things can come out of even the worst situations. A person may find their dream job after getting fired the week before. It sucks but if it that obstacle didn't happen, the other door wouldn't have opened. Even though the memory of a fragile 13 year old getting embarrassed and feeling worthless haunts me, I only became the coach and father I am because that happened. I'm not trying to be a Tony Robbins motivational speaker, but simply just explaining how I view moments in life. I learned to embrace the moments of love, joy, tears and even pain. I guess that's the only way I could continue to move forward and keep my sanity. If I didn't, then I may still be that 13 year old stuck in time.

I believe the people that read my story may be able to understand what I'm talking about. Unfortunately, I feel for the younger generation because they may have their head down and not even notice the little girl that sat next to them. Moments happen and we can't run or hide from it. Good or bad we just have to embrace the moments as they come.

Just as the great words of wisdom from the iconic Ferris Bueller, "Life moves pretty fast and if you don't stop and look around once in a while, you could miss it"….another one of my all-time favorites. Our lives take many paths throughout our lifetime. And the moments we encounter guide us along the journey. This particular journey began with the moment a 13 year old had his spirits shattered on the practice field to ultimately shedding tears of joy while being crowned Champion on the football field. To all those that helped and contributed to this moment and memory, I truly thank you for sharing the journey with me.

This was one of my life's lesson…one of my memories…this was one of my moments.

1993 PAL MIDGET DIVISION CHAMPIONS!!!

FINAL STATS
TOTAL POINTS COUGARS – 232
TOTAL POINTS OPPONENTS – 27
SACKS – 43
INTERCEPTIONS – 19
FUMBLES – 27
DEFENSE POINTS SCORED – 36

Undefeated 11 - 0

1993 Berryessa Cougars Team Roster

1 – Toby Torres	51 – Daniel Guiterrez
5 – Jonathan Pennywell	55 – Andrew Espino
7 – Steven Medina	56 – Steven Ochoa
10 – Joaquin Rivera	58 – Robert Fernandez
16 – Lawrence Serrano	66 – Peter Rea
17 – Rise Semela	68 – Michael Olson
20 – Oscar Martinez	75 – Charles Territo
24 – David Salinas	77 – Rudy Montalbo
27 – Eugene Dukes	80 – Damien Thomas
29 – Brandon Lattimore	81 – Frank Bermudez
32 – Ronal Moffett	84 – Daniel Navarro
34 – Charles Hobbs	87 – Hasani White
37 – Jermaine Green	89 – Javinni McLaughlin
40 – Asm Quresh	90 – William Lopez
41 – Justin Gonzales	91 – Gabriel Jimeniz
42 – Richard Garcia	94 – Richard Navarro
44 – Kevin Riley	99 – Rashad Jones

Head Coach – Ken Pruitt
Dave Andona – Assistant Coach
Larry Lee – Assistant Coach
Anthony Lombardi – Defensive Coordinator
Joe Melendez – Assistant Coach
Pablo Ochoa – Assistant Coach
Ricky Pruitt – Assistant Coach "aka Advisor"
Darrel Thomas – Assistant Coach